symbiotic
BUSINESS

HOW NONPROFITS AND FOR-PROFITS CAN CHANGE THE WORLD TOGETHER

BETTY L. CAMPBELL

EDITED BY TAMMY MOORE

Symbiotic Business: How Nonprofits and For-Profits Can Change the World Together
Copyright © 2022 by Betty L. Campbell

Published by
Legacy Layne Publishing
Hillsboro, Oregon

Edited by Tammy Moore
Book design by YellowStudios
Author headshot by Gochenour Photography

Paperback ISBN: 978-1-7378121-0-4
Library of Congress Control Number: 2021917701

Printed in the United States of America

This book is dedicated to my family, who stood by me from my early writing years through the delivery of my first book.

I also would like to acknowledge David Josephson, who taught me about the importance of networking, and who left me with the words, "If someone hands you the mic, take it." ringing in my memory.

I must also tip my hat to my coaches, Darcey Edwards, an incredible coach, mentor and inspiration, and Richard Zielke, who combines the nonprofit and for-profit worlds in an amazing and professional manner.

Contents

Foreword   **i**

Introduction   **1**

1: Giving Is Fundamental to Business   **5**

2: Giving Will Change You   **7**

I Want To Help, But How?   8

3: Your Customers Want to Give   **11**

4. Have It Your Way   **13**

Create a foundation   14

Create a Nonprofit Charity   15

5. Where to Start—Go Small   **17**

Local Is Valued   19

6. Choosing Your Nonprofits   **21**

Not All Charities Are Equal   22

7. Fiscal Responsibility   **25**

Follow Your Customers   27

8. Curating Your Portfolio—The Three Keys   **29**

Key 1: Heart Led Giving   30

Key 2: Touchpoints in the Community   31

Key 3: Connect Giving to Your Business Model   32

9. Giving Without Cash   **35**

Represent!   36

Encourage Employees to Join in!   38

10. It's Okay to Ask, "Where's Mine"   **39**

Board positions   40

11. It's About Community   **43**

12. Nonprofits, You Have a Stake in This!   **45**

13. We are Not Islands   **49**

Connecting Through Networking   50

Make It Personal   51

14. Start Small   **53**

Take the Mic   55

Don't Wait   56

15. It Begins One on One   **59**

16. How to Provide a Referral   **63**

Follow Up is Crucial   65

17. Quality Vs Quantity   **67**

18. Be Consistent   **69**

Give Back Outside of Your Purpose   70

19. Helping Through Social Media   **73**

20. Showing Appreciation to Business Donors   **75**

21. You Are Integral to the Community   77

22. We are Important to one Another   79

Acknowledgments   83

About Betty   87

   Connect with Betty   88

   Work with Betty   88

Foreword

When my good friend, Betty Campbell, asked me to write this foreword, I was honored. We have had many conversations about the foundational value all business must have: positive relationships. In this small volume, she has compiled information that not only describes the symbiotic relationship between the for-profit and the nonprofit worlds, but she has gone the next step in providing hands-on suggestions for both. I wish I had this book to guide me when I was an executive director of a nonprofit serving families who were homeless during the recession of the 1980s. It would have saved me a lot of head and heartache as well as provided wisdom I sorely needed.

I learned from those early mistakes, being fortunate to have had mentors who picked me up and helped move on to my current position as a business coach. I now work with new start-up businesses and within the nonprofit world as well, being on the Executive Committee of Nehemiah E-Community. I have watched Betty lead Xpose Hope over the past few years, but more importantly, I have watched her give back to her community in the form of the All About Business and All About...(various cities in our region) groups. In *Symbiotic Business* you will find that Betty draws from her own business experience as well as her experience leading a nonprofit to give us a full understanding of the symbiotic relationship: how businesses can give back to their communities and why they should; and how nonprofits need to be visible in the business community, not just to seek donors but to gain the visibility necessary to draw their volunteers with like-passioned people, develop mutual referral relationships, and support for their own organizational needs.

As you have opened this book, you have some interest in either furthering your company's involvement in your community or are trying to figure out how to be a nonprofit presence in your community. You will find in these pages helpful suggestions to fulfill both of those inquiries. And after she gives us that information, she presents a challenge for us, for-profit and nonprofit businesses, to dream big together. Who knows what those relationships are going to produce?

Richard Zielke
Zielke Coaching Solutions
& Nehemiah E-Community

Introduction

For-profit business and nonprofits are both businesses. Both keep a balance sheet. Both employ people. Both add diversity and function to the community. They often use one another; the nonprofit approaching businesses for donations and the for-profit model using their donations to gain tax advantages. But there can be so much more— that much more is relationship.

There are more than 1.3 million charitable nonprofits in the United States. They help our communities and they help fulfill our dreams in the hope of helping others. The premise is more than giving and taking; they bring us together to serve.

Nonprofits are everywhere — they are part of us. But we don't think of some of these organizations as charities. Churches, the YMCA, many hospitals, youth organizations, many of our community service agencies, most zoos, many education institutions, are not-for-profit!

As a consumer, much buying power is within the non-profit pocketbook. Every nonprofit utilizes numerous businesses in their community just to accomplish their mission. Employment agencies, bookkeepers, toilet paper vendors, and automotive repair companies benefit from the existence of nonprofits. Yes, charities impact our economy positively, in the same way for-profit businesses have changed our society. Our human experience has been changed because someone dared to ask "what if," and created a new product or service. The computer I'm using to write this volume is an example. A foldable kayak was invented because getting a kayak off the roof of a vehicle is too difficult for some people. The LED light has changed the way we light our homes and businesses. Innovation continues to push us forward.

So how do for-profit and nonprofit businesses move and merge in society together? We need innovation, and we need to believe that we can change the world for the better.

Our relationship is truly symbiotic. We need one another. Businesses that give attract the public by showing that they care. While helping other people, they lessen tax liability. When they give, they can help humanity move forward.

Nonprofits benefit from receiving the advice and wisdom from businesses who are outside in order to grow. They are greatly helped with financial donations and connections to multiple resources with people who care. They need to be seen.

This type of investment in one another can be considered relationship equity. If you have built up a lot of collateral in advance, other members of the community will invest back into you and into your business.

By working together to support and invest in each other, for-profit and not-for-profit ventures can grow together. We can change the world in so many ways, together. Tomorrow can be one of putting all of our pieces of time, treasure and talent on the table to make one spectacular puzzle.

Giving Is Fundamental to Business

"Think of giving not as a duty,
but as a privilege."
— John D. Rockefeller Jr.

Melissa Blackburne owns Sparkling Perfection House Cleaning. She's been at it a few years, and the business is growing. Her staffing needs have increased, and she considers herself a community-minded business.

"I give a lot...in fact, I have had to tighten up our pricing structure. My heart goes out to people, and I often discount when I shouldn't."

It's easy to find ourselves giving extensively, but questioning if we are making an impact on the world around us. Giving is so important, in fact, it has been the theme of multiple business books and manuals. One of the largest networking organizations in the world, BNI, uses the tagline "Givers Gain." A very well-known book called "The Go-Giver" became so popular that it spawned an educational series for high schools, and at least four other volumes!

Giving is part of the marketing pie. If the slices are things like Chamber and other networking memberships, social media, speaking, online marketing, events, and print, radio and television advertising, one of the pieces that is often forgotten as marketing is donations to nonprofits.

But, how does business give, how much, how often, and to whom? How do you help the community without giving away the farm? What channels are the best to allow your giving to also grow your business?

Most businesses are fastidious about perfecting their social media ads, keeping their expenses low and increasing sales. But many small businesses forget to use that same focus when it comes to giving. It's time to take the reigns of your business donations, and let them work strategically for you!

Giving Will Change You

"For it is in giving that we receive."
— St. Francis of Assisi

Studies done with the elderly show that those who volunteered lived longer, such as the study at University of California, Berkley, led by Doug Oman that showed the aged who volunteered for two or more organizations were 44% less likely to die over a five-year period than their counterparts.

A joint study completed in 2006 by Johns Hopkins University and the University of Tennessee showed that those who help actually had lower blood pressure than those in the study who did not volunteer.

When we give, oxytocin, a hormone that helps regulate and create strong relationships, is released. We feel connected, we are more content.

A study by Jorge Moll and his colleagues (National Institutes of Health) discovered that giving to charities actually activates endorphins that bring pleasure and happiness.

I Want To Help, But How?

You may have already been part of the business networking community for years. As a business owner, you have undoubtedly learned how to connect with other businesses. A plumber is a great referral for a real estate agent, a web designer might be a great referral for a chiropractor. But how do businesses provide referrals for nonprofits?

The most obvious answer is by listening. Find out how the charity began. Is it being run by its founder? If not, how did your connection become involved? Inquire as to their personal life, and then ask, "What connections do you need?" Perhaps they need to be invited to *your* networking groups!

As with your own business, you'll find that these needs change with time. Maybe they need to be connected to a home builder so they can provide housing, or perhaps they need a good social media person. Locations and services for fundraising events are always great connections.

Perhaps on a personal note, your networking partner just needs a house cleaner to help him stay on top of things.

Reconnect from time to time to check in, just as you would with any other referral partner.

Your Customers Want to Give

*"We make a living by what we get, we
make a life by what we give."*
— Winston S. Churchill

...And they want you to help them. Being altruistic is good for the community but it is good for the business, as well. Let's consider the recent phenomenon of Tom's Footwear.

Tom's created a very simple canvas shoe and offered it in several colors. The shoe itself was not phenomenal. In fact, it was very basic in terms of fashion. Created from a simple Argentinian boat shoe style, with no arch, and being fabric, they weren't created to last as long as a basic tennis shoe created from leather.

But Tom's created a consumer revolution when it offered to give a pair of shoes to someone in a third world country for each pair that was purchased.

The shoes that were donated were not as nice as the shoes they were marketing, but that didn't matter. Consumers from every age group rushed out to purchase shoes from Tom's, and they became a craze. Celebrities wore them and magazine articles were written about them. They were used in fashion shows and touted on talk radio.

They were all the rage because if you were going to buy shoes anyway, why not buy from someone who was helping to change the world by giving back?

Customers wanting to be part of a movement can be contagious. They will seek out businesses to support who are giving back to humanity. They don't care that the tax credit for the generosity goes to the business, and not to them. They don't care that their name will never be on a donor plaque. People who enjoy giving, generally do so, out of a desire to be part of something bigger than themselves.

Inventing ways for you to give through the efforts or purchases of your clients is a win-win-win, for you, for them, and for the charity!

Have It Your Way

*"No one has ever become poor
by giving."*
— Anne Frank

Many companies prefer to be very hands-on with their giving. It will help to gain publicity when the charitable cause you are giving to is controlled by your business. You don't have to request to be put on the charity website— it belongs to you. You don't have to worry that your name will be left off the donor list.

There are two simple ways to control the giving, and they work for many companies. However, if your business is in the beginning stages, you will probably find the added overhead of these methods to be more work that the write off is worth.

Create a foundation

One way to make a mark on the world is to create a foundation. Foundations are nonprofits that endow their financial gifts to other nonprofits. They can be very specific, such as a cancer foundation, or a children's foundation. Some are very general, such as a community foundation that may offer grants or loans to hundreds of small nonprofits in the community.

Many companies and business people begin foundations to control their giving. From the Gates Foundation, to the Mary Kay Ashe Foundation, to the DoTerra Healing Hands Foundation, these organizations provide funding to countless other nonprofits.

Foundations allow your business to be seen as altruistic, and to show compassion for many areas of need in your community. A foundation can get press for funding a children's play in the community one week, and for funding a blanket drive the next. It's a great way to control what organizations who you are giving to, do with the funds that you provide. Grants are often project specific, so you can give to a homeless shelter for a program that helps the homeless learn a skill, or to a food bank to provide reusable bags to assist in the elimination of litter.

Grants can only be used as directed by the grantor, or the funds must be returned to the granting organization. This provides a great deal of power to the grantor, and ensures the funds provided for feeding the elderly, for example, won't be used on marketing campaigns or staff development. Most grants also have stipulations that an end of spending report be sent to the granting agency, providing specifics on how the funds were utilized.

Create a Nonprofit Charity

American Family Insurance chose to create their own community initiative to help others pursue their dreams. Their DreamBank digital experience supports those who need information and encouragement to begin a business or change their communities for the better.

Events include lunchtime yoga offerings, women's initiatives, motivational workshops and imagination prods. Through the Dreams Foundation, grants are provided to nonprofits, and the entire program is nestled in the American Family Insurance website.

Many brands have ventured into the world of creating a charity. Then, there are brands that are created to be a charity, such as Newman's Own, a food brand that was launched by actor Paul Newman. Newman's own was created to give 100% of its net profit to charity. Since 1982, according to the company website, more than $550 million has been donated. That is quite an impact, and the company employs a sizable workforce.

Where to Start—Go Small

"I am a little pencil in the hand of a writing God who is sending a love letter to the world."

— Mother Teresa

Small nonprofits are often the backbone of a community. In addition, they are generally unique in their purposes, and local in their area of emphasis. Not only are they homegrown, and therefore easy to get to know, they are also generally more apt to provide reverse advertising to a small business or a possible advisory board position. The buy-in to their annual events will be less, and their presence in the community may be stronger than a branch of a national organization.

In Waldport, Oregon, a small co-op finds, repairs, and paints bicycles green. These bikes are left out for the community to utilize, free of charge. They are parked, and can be taken by another person, which keeps the community rolling along, both figuratively and literally.

The organization is staffed by volunteers, and many children in the Waldport area attribute their first bicycle ride to a green bicycle. In addition, tourists utilize them, with some families looking forward to their time in the coastal town just for the experience of riding the green bikes.

Another great organization is Rockin' Rooms, created by a mother named Valerie Morton, whose son was fighting cancer. Her son spent an immense amount of time in the hospital. Although the pediatric wards are painted in brighter colors, any room occupied by a child with a compromised immune system, and unable to leave for weeks, can become very boring. She realized quickly that gifts of quilts, posters, games, and toys were very welcome and comforting. These items transformed the rooms from looking like sterilized institutional settings into a softer place of comfort with the flavor of home. The distraction allowed a child to be a child again, playing games, and rambling on about their favorite theme, be it princesses, or super-heroes. Morton's charitable organization provides for hundreds of children per year, brightening their stays and offering comfort and hope.

There are probably many small organizations like these in your vicinity. A good way to find nonprofits which may resonate with you and your business is by asking your chamber of commerce, your local licensing department or checking your state's nonprofit registries. A good non-profit consultant can help you to distinguish between active and inactive charities, as well as check out their track record and community impact.

Local Is Valued

We recognize the names of many national and interna-tional philanthropic organizations that are responsible for groundbreaking change. Even so, the world, however small it may seem, still centers around the local commu-nity for most of our customers. Their concerns focus on things like the need for new equipment for the local youth baseball league, the neighbor who was in a severe acci-dent or the homeless dogs on their street. As a business, knowing the concerns of your customers allows you to create relationship with them that encourages repeat business and loyalty to your brand.

Local nonprofits are the heartbeat of many communities, but they are often not receiving large grants. Grant writ-ing, in itself has become a specialty, and hiring a grant writer can be expensive. In addition, the donors of many small nonprofits are known by name in the community. They are appreciated and honored at events, in advertis-ing and on their websites. Small nonprofits are accustomed to working with small businesses who may not have tens of thousands to gift, but who still want to share their success with those in the community.

Choosing Your Nonprofits

"Charity begins at home but should not end there."

— Thomas Fuller

Giving is much easier when you are invested in the community that the charity serves. If you have a family member who is fighting cancer, then a local group that cleans the homes of cancer patients could be an excellent recipient of your donations. Perhaps you are an artist and want to give to a local art guild, or a program that provides funds for art classes in local schools.

However, you might also want to match your giving to your business type. A builder, for instance, may want to give to a local organization that does home repairs for senior citizens, helps a high school shop class, or a collaborative that is working to fund parks in the area for children to play.

Let's examine some important points to consider when choosing to align with a charity, so that the relationship can be beneficial to both you and to the organizations you choose!

Not All Charities Are Equal

Not all charities receive the same consideration when grants are being allocated. Larger charities can keep funds rolling in through hired grant writers, and their budget often includes funding for tv, social media and radio advertisements.

Your donation dollars have a lot of competition with such organizations. Your business will likely not gain the same kind of acknowledgement, notoriety and loyalty as it would to the local community it serves.

However, smaller local charities often struggle for resources. Often, their staff is unpaid, but these grassroot community organizations often do the lion's share of community work. Across the country, small organizations gather to clean the homes of cancer patients, to provide hats for those in chemo, to hold premature babies in hospitals, or to create after school snacks in underprivileged schools.

In addition, many of these locally created groups welcome business owners onto their governing and advisory boards. They seek the advice that businesses can provide, and they are willing to give community affirmation in return.

Fiscal Responsibility

*"Where there is charity and wisdom,
there is neither fear nor ignorance."*
— Francis of Assisi

When a company gives, the donations can literally provide life to a trafficked woman, or they can be spent on a personal refrigerator. How can a donor know that the funds provided are not being squandered?

Several safeguards are built into the not-for-profit system. The most obvious is the IRS. All charities listed as 501©3 businesses with the Internal Revenue Service must file a review of their finances annually. The IRS can and does make financial audits of nonprofits much like it does for other businesses. Most states also require some type of reporting from nonprofits each year, as well.

Guidestar is an organization that assists donors in following the financial operations of nonprofits. Guidestar rates the organizations, listing how resources are utilized; they provide information on percentages of revenue spent on staff, on programs and on supplies.

Charities which earn less than $50,000 per year fill out a post card, with very basic information. Therefore, systems like GuideStar do not have enough information to provide a true picture of an organization. However, any donor is able to request a copy of the books and receive the information. Most very small organizations don't have the assets to provide an annual report, however, when a bookkeeper is hired, an annual report should be available.

Books are easy to manipulate, so the best way to check a charitable organization is to be intimately involved with it. Then you will recognize clues that the executive director requesting or acknowledging donations of items that do not seem related to the mission stated in their bylaws?

A children's foster care charity probably has little need for a ski boat, for instance. Do donations seem to go to personal care of one of the board members? Are they asking for money to keep going financially (personally) so they can run the organization?

Some grace must be given, however, for small organizations who are operating with a volunteer treasurer as they start up. Don't expect the detailed reports that you'd receive from a large national organization each year. Being present with the board members and the charity will help you see if your donations are providing the desired outcomes.

Follow Your Customers

A great way to find an inroad and connect with a business account that has been difficult to attain, is to find out what nonprofits might be endorsed by that business. Attending auctions, golf tournaments and annual events, showing that you share their concerns for those saving the historic theater, chronic illness charities, environmental organizations or the homeless can open up conversations.

Many of these events involve a plethora of business leaders. Your business can be seen as an important community leader when it involves itself in giving efforts. Not every charity function you attend needs to be for one of your sponsored organizations. As the executive director of a nonprofit, even I attend the galas of other nonprofits, so that I can raise my visibility in the community and support the vision of other charities.

Curating Your Portfolio—
The Three Keys

*"Those who are happiest are those who
do the most for others."*
— Booker T. Washington

Much like an investment portfolio, a well-rounded offering of community initiatives and giving helps to keep your company in the public eye, and also assures a connection to more customers. One easy recipe is: 1/3 heart led, 1/3 business connected, and 1/3 community driven.

As a business, I suggest considering these three keys when choosing nonprofits with which to be aligned. These keys could very well be the pathway to reach new customers in your business venture, while helping you selectively choose targets in your giving strategies: Your Heart, Your Community, Your Business Model.

This three-pronged approach is so exciting and important! It allows you to reach three different segments of your community while you enjoy the satisfaction of giving in a way that fuels your passion, bolsters your business, and serves the community.

For example, if you are a builder who has a heart for the men and women who have served in the military, perhaps you can align with an organization that provides home repairs to disabled veterans.

Key 1: Heart Led Giving

When launching a business, you likely considered what type of business fueled your passion—one that would have you jumping out of bed each morning and hit the ground running with all cylinders.

This segment is perhaps the easiest to encourage an entrepreneur with feeling connection. A parent of a child with autism may find small agencies in the local area that serve children with special needs. At least one will tug at the heart strings enough to garner donations.

A woman who has escaped the cycle of abuse will know who helped her—a local charity that provides housing, or a free counseling center, for example. She'll want to give back where she was helped.

What difficulties did you overcome in your life, and how can you provide help to others who are now encountering those same issues? Did you find perhaps, that there weren't adequate resources when you were at your lowest point, so you want to help create those helping hands?

Key 2: Touchpoints in the Community

Many communities have certain causes which it embraces; a well-loved coach stricken with cancer, a watershed that is being polluted, an area impacted by a tornado— which the entire community mourns and rallies together for such causes.

Although large agencies like the Red Cross inevitably help with natural disasters, simply writing a check to them may not be a reminder to your community that you care about *them*. When events occur, look to see who is helping and what publicity they receive.

When fires hit a local community, a neighborhood insurance agent who specialized in serving farms, donated money, time and equipment to move farm animals out of harm's way.

His national company donated to the efforts of a small nonprofit he was working through, and both he and the community organization benefitted from his actions and the donation. The press covered the donation, including taking photos of a poster sized check, showing the man as something of a local hero, who was engaged and concerned

If you are based near an area of natural beauty like a beach, you could connect with a beach cleanup organization. You can provide financially so that the marketing for volunteers can be accomplished. In addition, you also might hand out collection bags with your logo, or offer to send employees during their normal work hours to assist in the cleanup.

Key 3: Connect Giving to Your Business Model

Giving back, in your business model not only makes financial sense, it also reminds your customers that although they are utilizing your service and/or products, that you are also invested in the needs of the community.

There are two ways to connect your business model to your donations.

The first is to connect with an organization that would assist in the education of those employees you would like to hire one day. A construction firm might connect with an organization to teach the trades to the underprivileged, for instance.

Another avenue that is similar, is linking to an organization that your product connects with, in the hope that your brand can become synonymous with the vision and mission of that nonprofit. If you sell high end bicycles then sponsoring charity bike rides would be a natural combination. You might also field a bike team to participate in the ride, and assist the organization with medals or certificates.

Giving Without Cash

*"Everyone can be great, because
everyone can serve."*
— Martin Luther King, Jr.

Not all businesses can afford to financially donate when they are in their infancy. However, all businesses have assets that can make a big difference to a small nonprofit. Providing copier usage, or assisting with a one-time event by offering tables, chairs or labor is extremely helpful to a small organization. Donating a used vehicle, or some used office equipment can help a new community group work more efficiently.

Labor donations can be staff who are on the clock with your business. Habitat for Humanity has built a business model on this type of philanthropy, encouraging businesses to send labor, and encouraging the homeowner to not only build on their property, but on the homes of other habitat recipients!

Your accounting department might be able to take a load off of a small nonprofit by keeping books and preparing taxes. If your business is in the technical field, providing computer repairs could save such an organization thousands of needed dollars.

Hosting a fundraiser or "get to know you" event is another excellent, very low cost way to give back! Most nonprofits are looking for new volunteers and donors, so a meet and greet in your business location, or at your golf course is a great way to help out.

Represent!

Advertising space to create awareness of any brand is expensive, but local charities often struggle to be known. It can take a decade to grow a nonprofit to the point that an annual gala will be profitable. But as a business, you have an incredible opportunity to assist in creating a spotlight.

Social media has created overnight successes of new ideas, new solutions and great small organizations. Simply mentioning one of your charities favorably, or beginning a social media fund raiser for a group can bring expanded notice, and hundreds of new donors.

Speaking in public, is a great time to mention one of your preferred organizations. You can mention it in networking meetings, or you can allow them a space at a table when you are selling books at a speaking engagement. Your company name being used to inform the community of an event can be incredibly valuable.

A great example was some of the assistance provided by businesses to nonprofits during the government's mandatory shut down. In one community, business owners came together to serve food for Meals on Wheels. In another, a large manufacturer offered space to open a new food bank.

We all need to advertise, but especially in social media situations, the basic "this is our brand... this is our product" ads can get old with your audience very quickly.

However, the community can't seem to get enough of hearing how people go out of their way to give back. One of the most popular series of posts in one of my community groups was a legal firm that was buying lunch once each week for essential workers. One week, they went to a grocery store and delivered pizza for the employees; another week, they brought subs to a fire station. The company, very wisely, involved the community in the selection process of each week's location.

Encourage Employees to Join in!

Perhaps your employees want to help their community, but it is as difficult for them to find suitable places, as it was for your company, to find the right places to donate. There are many ways to encourage community giving in the workplace.

Begin by offering to be a collection point for donations of small items. Perhaps the local shelter is in need of socks in the winter time. You can place bins for collection at the entrance to your offices, and allow the charity to pick up from your place of business. Encourage your employees to tell friends and neighbors, perhaps offering a prize to the employee donating the most items.

Encourage employees to give time to organizations by offering to pay for 2-5 hours a year donated to a local nonprofit. Encourage a few of the organizations that are in your local Chamber of Commerce to provide flyers that you can post for employees to choose from.

If you have the structure in place to do so, allow your employees to donate directly from their checks to nonprofits of their choosing. Many large corporations match these types of donations, or pay organizations a small amount per hour that one of their employees donates of their personal time. It is possible to do a funding drive for smaller firms, as well.

It's Okay to Ask, "Where's Mine"

"Giving to those in need will bring more joy than money could every buy."
— Dave Ramsey

Nonprofits realize that larger donors need to be finessed, and they will often have numerous options available to donors who participate frequently. The offering may be as simple as a business logo. However, larger donors are often provided board or advisory board positions, advertising on the charity website, or preferred seating and mention at events.

Board positions are excellent mechanisms to raise the awareness of you personally in the community, as well as your brand. Most boards meet only a few times a year, but being listed as an executive and a board member of a few nonprofits tells the community that you care, and you are invested in them.

Most board positions do require a buy in of a particular donation. If you have skills in finance, marketing or management, the charity as a whole will benefit from your knowledge, and you will in turn, gain from their constant exposure of board members. Such a position reflects well in resumes and LinkedIn profiles, increasing your personal stature in the community.

Make known your willingness to emcee or provide speaking services at events. Perhaps, introduce the winner of a particular award or talk about your experiences as a volunteer, raising the value of your participation.

Nonprofits should have marketing personnel who are attending local networking events. Even the smallest charity can generally afford to be part of the chamber or a small coffee networking group. Every nonprofit that you are supporting should be using their connections to provide referrals for you. If they aren't, get the marketing person a copy of "Symbiotic Business" to read!

Board positions

A hidden gem that is available for your resume and introductions is the board position. Nonprofits have operating boards that need to seat members, as well as advisory boards and committee positions that need to be filled.

Time is of the essence, of course, but most executive boards of smaller nonprofits meet only a few times a year. Committee positions are more work intensive, but if your heart is in the work, or if you are skilled in the area (fundraising, for example,) this can be a great outlet outside of your day-to-day business position.

Board positions allow you to speak into an organization with authority, and allow you to make a difference in the community. Your expertise is priceless to nonprofits! A member of a board or committee is more likely to endorse the organization publicly. That kind of publicity is priceless!

Most board positions do require a minimum yearly donation, smaller organizations will often allow you to pay that amount monthly.

It's About Community

*"Service to others is the rent you pay for
your room here on earth."*
— Mohammed Ali

Your family and your business exist within a realm that
includes nonprofits. Our lives are actually impacted by
charities more than it would seem at first glance. Giving
is a vital component of being in a position to receive. After
all, when we give, our hand is already open to receive.
Contributing to the care of others is an important part of
the human experience. The work that nonprofits do, can't
be duplicated in any cost-efficient way by government
agencies. It is because of the humanitarian work of charities that help keep taxes lower.

Caring for the elderly, taking veterans to chemotherapy
appointments, and offering groceries at food banks all
change the dynamic of our communities. They enhance

the environment in which families work and play. Your business is a piece of that puzzle, but without community services, so many vital pieces are missing from the picture. We help one another, give to one another, and together, bring growth. It's imperative for our future.

Nonprofits, You Have a Stake in This!

"We know only too well that what we are doing is nothing more than a drop in the ocean. But if the drop were not there, the ocean would be missing something."
— Mother Teresa

Cheryl is not looking forward to sitting down at her desk. The board has been breathing down her neck because she is a week behind on the donor update, and they are running low on patience, waiting for that email. But she is also in charge of the annual fun run, which must be successful in order to make budget.

Grants have been few and far between, and this morning, she needs to be at the Chamber of Commerce to beg for donations before launching all the advertising which will draw maximum participation. Unfortunately, she knows that a smaller cancer foundation has put their annual auction in for the same month. It's important that she outshine the other organization.

Even though she has a master's degree in nonprofit management, sales pitches aren't her thing. She knows how to institute programs and oversee budgets, but times have been tough, and this year speaking to groups and sealing the deal with donors and procuring donations has fallen on her.

It might be different if she really knew anyone at this meeting. At least she only has to visit the chamber the month prior to the event. After the fun run event she'll send a quick "thank you" to the chamber to be posted in their newsletter and they'll be happy to have assisted the children exiting abuse, who Cheryl's organization serves.

Running a nonprofit is a difficult occupation. The nonprofit world must still balance budgets, much like for profit businesses. The organization must remain in the black, employing staff while they are providing vital services to the community. In addition, there are new nonprofits popping up every day, all competing for the same fundraising dollars. When the economy falters, the donatable dollars decrease, so the pie that must be divided, shrinks. Unlike a for-profit business, Cheryl can't just ramp up production or add a new product line to increase sales.

Networking with businesses is an important part of the job, but many nonprofits don't understand the true value and depth of networking. Many colleges teach that networking is something that a nonprofit does only for upcoming events, and that it is nothing more than a well-timed sales pitch.

We are Not Islands

"At the end of the day, it's not about what you have or even what you've accomplished...it's about who you've lifted up, who you've made better. It's about what you've given back."
— Denzel Washington

Sometimes, those of us who work in the nonprofit world consider ourselves to be so different from for profit businesses that we segment ourselves out. In many areas, there are even chambers of commerce just for nonprofits. After all, our goal is to have everything that comes in, go out in the form of services and education. We aren't trying to bring money to our investors. In many ways, we are not shaped like for-profit ventures.

But we don't exist alone. The funding used to complete charitable tasks, needs to be constantly refreshed with new resources, while reaching new donors, much like our for-profit counterparts; those businesses must attend to current accounts while creatively reaching new customers. When local businesses are struggling, our donation base may consequently wither. Yes, our island is very connected to the mainland supply channels.

Connections can be created through several channels. Donor base often connects us to other businesses. Speaking engagements can assist in linking us, as can association membership (such as Kiwanis International®, Optimists International®, and Rotary International®.) However, the best way to create relationship with for-profit businesses is to participate in business networking groups.

Some of the best-known brands of networking groups nationally are BNI®, LeTip®, Women In Business®, and your local Chamber of Commerce.

Connecting Through Networking

True networking is more than selling products and services. It's all about connecting with people and building relationships. That means a long-term investment in the community around our organizations. In reality, for non-profits to function, they must learn to operate *within* the community, not merely *for* the community.

For instance, if I own a tea store, my product is tea, but I also connect with many other businesses that intersect with my own, such as the water department, the sugar distributor, and maybe the vendor of snacks to go with the tea. I might also consider connecting with the restaurant down the street as a place to come before or after dining, or with a limo service as a destination, or an Air BnB to be mentioned in their "around town" brochures.

I might want to know what type of clients these businesses want to attract and I might even go out of my way to refer a few clients to them. Those small acts of kindness cement my brand in their minds.

This is where nonprofits often get stuck. We often see our business as the service we provide, and our efforts at networking can become whittled down to nothing more than the task of finding donors. However, there is a huge business world out there that we, as executive directors, marketing executives, and nonprofit board members would benefit by connection to and serving!

Make It Personal

Networking is a portion of the marketing effort, but networking is a very personal experience and not every approach works for every connection. We as business people, are putting ourselves out into the marketplace to connect and create a sense of community. We are linking

arms one-on-one with those who serve our neighbor-
hoods in other ways; some by turning a profit and other
by providing options to those who have special needs, or
need assistance.

Networking is more than joining an organization. A good
friend and master networker friend once stated, "The
more you play, the more it pays." Networking is specific
to relationship. It is aimed at actually knowing and in-
vesting in people, not just reading their demographics
and throwing advertisements at them.

Start Small

"Alone we can do so little; together we can do so much."

— Helen Keller

If your organization is small with few or no paid staff, your main objective is serving your chosen area of expertise. You can't allow marketing, donors or networking to get in the way of the special work of your organizational focus. You may not have an abundance of staff hours to spend on networking, and it is perfect to just begin with a single networking group to connect you to others.

Your local chamber of commerce is a great starting point. Most chambers will teach a new member how to network, and will try to make connections for you. If your chamber has a weekly networking meeting, you may find it beneficial to attend. Wear a name badge so that you are easy to locate in the room. Though it may seem very last century, carry plenty of business cards.

Who should you connect in these first meetings? Everyone. When I began in nonprofit world, I was cautious, trying to connect only to those businesses I knew donated large amounts to charities. I later realized that every person in that room was closely acquainted with about 100 more, and loosely connected with up to 1,000 other people. What a great sales force potential to have preaching your message to the world!

I learned to focus, not on selling my nonprofit and our needs, but on listening to people and hearing their stories. Every person has stories, whether that is how they started or what is currently going on in their personal lives. Often, I found that their epic journey and my personal story intersected somewhere. That intersection is fertile ground to plant the seed of relationship.

I learned that Martha's mom had the same cancer that my late husband had courageously battled. I found that Robert moved to the area from the same city I had lived for thirty years. I heard the story of the attorney who worked his way up from a broom closet runner position, to a law degree, and I connected with a member of city council over our concern for kids in the community.

As you connect to others, those contacts will connect their friends and business acquaintances to you. They will also want to get to know you and your passion, and in turn, will be another resource to help your mission succeed.

These connections don't come free of charge, however. You also need to be considering who you know, and with whom they may also be introduced, extending and enlarging the circle of influence and connection. You need to learn to make gracious introductions, and follow up on those connections.

Take the Mic

When I first began networking, a good friend and mentor once told me that I was burying my message. I didn't understand what he meant. "When you are given the opportunity to take the mic, you often turn it over to someone else. Being a nonprofit doesn't mean your input is not important. Take the mic."

From that day forward, I began to act as if I were the expert in human trafficking. That wasn't hard, because in reality, I was an insider who'd spent my days immersed in that world. I know more about traffickers, the adult industry, and what it takes to get out than nearly anyone in my metropolitan area.

When trafficking victims want to leave that life, I can provide the resources needed to get out. I know what the risks are for their children. I keep on top of the legislation that is currently being considered, and if those changes will hurt or help. I truly am the expert in my nonprofit's arena of service.

I also know the best pizza in town, how to hire the right attorney and I can help you find a great company who can fix your air conditioner. I'm an expert in many things, so I should take the microphone when asked, and I should add my input. If a radio station called and offered a free 30 second spot, I wouldn't hesitate to provide a quick advertisement timed to the second. So why wouldn't I use speaking opportunities in my networking community to expand my organization's reach?

Don't Wait

The reason a lot of businesses, both for-profit and non-profit don't take those speaking opportunities is that they are not prepared in advance. Don't wait until someone asks you to give a one-minute or ten-minute presentation. Get ready now.

Prepare a PowerPoint® presentation for a longer talk. In fact, I keep three on hand at all times, in addition to at least five one-minute presentations that I can pull up on my phone for reminders.

Practice these short talks in front of a mirror. Practice with your family. Smile, breathe, and present.

It Begins One on One

*"If you need to raise funds from donors,
you need to study them, respect them
and build everything you do
around them."*

— Jef Brooks

Networking provides so much more than donors. Every
nonprofit needs a constant flow of volunteers, input from
professionals, and advice. Through networking, the nonprofit I work for has received donations of product,
connections to a volunteer bookkeeper, and free dental
care for our clients.

In networking, begin by asking, "Tell me about you."
When I ask this, often the person will relate information
about their business. After they wind down in that description, I say, "Now...tell me about you!"

I want to know who they are. Where is their heart? What are their interests? Are they a parent? Did they move about the country when they were young? What is their favorite sport? As you begin to know them as people, you can better know who in your sphere of contacts, can support their endeavors; more than their business, though it includes their work life, as well.

Then ask, "What are your most pressing needs? Who do you need to meet?" They may need a great chiropractor who specializes in helping people with headaches or they might need to offload their human resource work to an outside vendor.

After listening and giving resources and referrals, tell the story of your nonprofit. When I tell the story of Xpose Hope, I am confident that they will be encouraged to serve back. Most importantly, I explain why I have decided to become involved in my nonprofit, why it speaks to my heart, and why I believe we impact the community for the good. Your "why's" are a huge connection between you and your network.

I am careful to give case references, but not true names. Protect your clients, but place them as the center of the conversation, so that they will be remembered. Sometimes, I personally like to show before and after photos. I want to connect on a very personal level; the person I'm meeting with, to the people I serve. I want them to have empathy, and to remember the girls I have rescued when a giving opportunity arises.

I don't ask them to give the first time we connect. I'm just building a relationship by listening to them and telling them about what we do. I never want to be "that non-profit" that always has its hands out. I strive to be different. I want them to believe what we do is so important that their business and their personal lives would be enhanced by helping us. That may be monetarily, service, or it may be connections. Perhaps, my desire to be different than other nonprofits, is that I also look for ways to promote the businesses that are willing to give back or pay it forward, as they are able.

It makes sense, doesn't it, that personal connection will bring more results and more long-term donors than form letters and social media posts. Most charities provide personal services of some type, whether that is helping to feed shut-ins, providing medical care, giving a service or counseling. Of all businesses, nonprofits should easily recognize the importance of a trusted personal relationship.

How to Provide a Referral

"As you grow older, you will discover that you have two hands—one for helping yourself, the other for helping others."
— Audrey Hepburn

When you first begin networking, you may feel over-whelmed with giving referrals. You may not think you have a lot of connections to share. However, through the art of listening you will find that you are more capable than you may have first imagined.

For instance, the web designer in your group may be looking for those in the dental field to share his services with. You may not have been networking for years, but you probably have a personal dentist. Next time you are in the chair, just tell him you appreciate his service and hope your friends have an easy time finding him, too. Ask if it is alright to provide his contact information with a friend who does web design with no obligation.

Perhaps someone on your board of directors is an attorney, specializing in estates. What a perfect connection for someone in the hospice field, or someone working with widows, or someone who recently started a business and needs to plan for the future!

Providing that referral is as simple as writing a joint email to the two parties. I generally describe both of the people, and make a quick introduction. For instance:

"Dear Jim and Stacey, I recently had coffee with Jim, and I was so impressed with his concern for his clients, and his innovative strategies that I thought might be of benefit to you! Jim is one of our advisory board members, and I know you like to work with people who are giving back to the community.

Jim, let me introduce Stacey, who runs Gidgets and Gadgets. She is an amazing go-getter, who has built her business from the inception of an idea to a rock-solid business, expanding with multiple locations. She was mentioning her need of someone to assist with her growing accounting needs. I wanted to introduce you!"

Because we all value working with people who come with a great reputation, this type of connection is very helpful to both parties. Both will appreciate the time you put into creating a relationship with them, and with each other. In turn, usually, they will want to assist in helping your business to grow as well!

Follow Up is Crucial

For a business person providing a connection or referral, value and respect their reputation, as you do with your nonprofit's. When a company provides a link, it is extremely important to follow up quickly and professionally.

It is simple to create a database for your referrals, with basic information such as the referral's name, business, email and phone number, as well as who referred them to you. Update that database when you reach out, and keep track of the outcome of the connections.

It's also appropriate to send a quick note or email thanking the person referring, for thinking of you, and creating that avenue of gratitude.

Another important part of follow up is to attend important events of those with whom you network. This creates a personal connection, and it tells them that, what matters to them is also important to you, as well.

Quality Vs Quantity

"We need to value donors as much as we need value from them."

— Reinier Spruit

Statistically speaking, there are those who will tell you the number of businesses you connect with weekly is a sign of your growth. True, more connection can lead to greater innovation and expansion. It means more potential generated resources. However, producing a harvest of corn is more than throwing corn kernels into a field. Watering, fertilizing and protecting seeds after they are planted is necessary. Crops aren't ready for harvest overnight. It.... Takes.... time.

Networking is similar. Getting to know someone takes more time than spending a few moments with them. Properly formatted, a one-to-one has three sections; the preparation, the personal meeting, and the follow up.

Prior to meeting, it is important to do a little research. Look into the company that your network partner is part of, how long have they existed and what makes them different from their competition. Then check them out—social media is a great help here. Not only are there personal sites like Facebook®, Instagram®, MeWe®, and Gab®, there are also business styled social media platforms such as LinkedIn® and Alignable®. Both of these have paid versions, but you can usually glean the information you need using only a free account. (By the way, I suggest that you have an account in both of those, if you don't already.) Use this research to formulate a few questions for your meeting.

After the meeting, be certain to provide any resources you promised, including referrals. I usually do this in a follow up email, thanking the individual for spending time with me, and for taking the time to hear my story. I often provide links to other businesses, book referrals, or apps that I have found to be very helpful.

A month after this, I will send a follow up email to ask, "do you have new needs? I hope that we will be able to meet again soon!"

Be Consistent

"In any team sport, the best teams have consistency and chemistry."
— Roger Staubach

Imagine if your group provided lunch in the park for underprivileged children every Saturday at noon. But, let's say, one Saturday you didn't feel like it, or were sidetracked with a large event coming up and you didn't arrive with your totes full of lunch bags. That would be confusing and disheartening to your clients. They need to know that they can count on you to be part of their process. They need to be able to trust that you are consistently there for them.

Many nonprofits are members of local chambers of commerce. However, many don't attend weekly meetings or events. They seldom provide someone to serve as a chamber ambassador or committee member. The general practice is for a 501c3 to show up a few weeks before a Bike-A-Thon, or a charity auction, and rally for everyone to attend.... "We really need your support!"

There is often a video with a few client interviews, or a story that tugs at the heart. Everyone wants to help...and they sign up to run ten miles, bowl, or buy a dinner. When that event is complete, the organization stops attending the meetings.

While this may infuse an organization with some quick cash, it isn't building long-term donors or support in the community through relationships. Consistent participation and becoming an integral part of your networking organizations will provide so much more gain in the long run. It also raises your presence with those who are building the businesses around you. It connects you, long-term with philanthropists and volunteers. It allows you to assist other charities who are also vitally important to the puzzle.

Give Back Outside of Your Purpose

Not-for-profit ventures are formed as a way to give resources to the community. Sometimes, we can become laser focused on that purpose and forget that without those around us, growth is limited. A 200- piece puzzle is only so big when completed. when you buy a 1000-piece puzzle, in contrast, it is much larger and is generally more detailed. Incorporating "the many" into your vision through connection is much like the 1000-piece puzzle. It is more far reaching, has more growth, and benefits a greater number.

A homeless outreach that also takes cases of water or snacks to the local fire or police department stands to gain more from that gesture through social media, news media and goodwill than they would from some marketing campaigns.

Partnering with a for-profit business to do a fundraiser helps both organizations. The business is able to be introduced to new clients, and the charity finds a donated location or event. In turn, more people learn how the organization impacts their community while connecting with potential new donors. Craft workshops, food tastings, sporting events and more, lend themselves to partnership opportunities.

Creating space for businesses to grow can create the kind of goodwill that brings in donations and volunteers as well. Xpose Hope created local Facebook pages for the communities in which it serves. Those sites are open to posts from community members and businesses alike. Small companies have increased in size due to the ability to advertise there without charge, and volunteers have provided apparel, hands on assistance and services to our outreach.

Based on the community excitement around those sites, we also began to host a complementary business networking group. Instead of paying for the opportunity to be in the meetings, donations to our organization are encouraged. The ties that have been formed within that group literally carried us through a national emergency. The investment was only a bit more than an hour of time per week and a free Facebook group. At a time when a large segment of small businesses was struggling to survive, the payoff has been substantial.

Helping Through Social Media

*"Happiness doesn't result from what we
get, but from what we give."*
— Ben Carson

Your social media account is a platform which you can utilize, personally and professionally, to assist local companies in getting their message out. Simply liking and interacting with local business posts helps their algorithms so that more eyes see their messaging.

However, you can also post on your personal social media (which isn't really personal if you are in business) when you attend events with, or utilize the services of local shops. Pictures tell the story; you don't even need many words.

During the Covid response, the nonprofits in Hillsboro, Oregon were brainstorming ways to keep one another going. One of the local nonprofits, Bag & Baggage Productions, created videos for all the local charities. They ran those on their social media platforms and allowed us to forward them. This brought in new donations and visibility to the organizations, and connected them all through mutual support.

In return, the organizations they assisted, spread the news far and wide about the theater company's relaunch into performances.

Showing Appreciation to Business Donors

"Be hearty in your approbation and lavish in your praise."
— Dale Carnegie

Nonprofits so often hone in clients only to forget that they also serve the entire community. Our business connections need to feel that your organization has importance to them as well as to the intended clients.

Written notes provided twice a year go a long way, touching base with those who provide facilities, connection or funding. In today's world, the hand-signed note, even if it is computer generated, exudes a special air of care.

Noting your larger donors on your website, and including their logo (make them clickable!) increases their brand awareness and shows that the community invests in your cause.

Small gifts that say "You matter to us, personally," such as a booklet on business advice, (even if it is written by your executive director or a board member) or workshops designed for donors on subjects such as lowering stress, means a lot to those who volunteer or donate.

You Are Integral to the Community

"I've learned that you shouldn't go through life with a catcher's mitt on both hands. You need to be able to throw something back."
— Maya Angelou

Yes, charities do serve the community. We are also part of the community we serve. We might live there. We definitely work there, and our clients are served there. It is imperative that we remember that we are only one piece in a puzzle that isn't complete without us, and we cannot see the entire picture without all the other pieces connecting.

One of the best parts about my work with Xpose Hope has been that when I walk into a business, they know who I am. They feel connected to me, and I am concerned for them. I want their business and their family to thrive. I know that we are so much better together.

Becoming an integral part of the picture may change your nonprofit forever. You can realize benefits; both personal and professional. You may come to see on a higher level that your work is appreciated and necessary. You will find that your efforts to grow become easier, and your ability to create change for your clients is expanded.

When we work with clients, we know that telling someone we have fed 400 families is good information, but we will get more support by telling the story of just one of those families. The businesses you will connect with are the same. They all have a story. Knowing those stories will change your life, and the life of your nonprofit. Bring your vibrance to your community. Be a vital link to others and you'll grow your business as well!

We are Important to One Another

"Coming together is a beginning, staying together is progress, and working together is success."
— Henry Ford

A community with no services for the elderly, means fewer can be in the work force while caring for their parents. This hampers the ability of business to grow.

A nonprofit cannot exist without volunteers, without donors and without a community to serve. We simply cannot exist without each other.

By serving one another, not as customers or tax write offs, but as important community members, we can change the portion of the world that we call home, and at times, make great change to the entire world.

But simply providing a handout does not create change. There is more to giving than writing a check. There is more to serving the community than the focus of a single nonprofit.

Understanding the needs of one another and knowing the heartbeat of our community, impacts everyone around us. It impacts the bottom line, it impacts our employees, and it impacts those who need a little help to get through sometimes—be that a veteran with a leaky roof, or a mom overwhelmed with a special needs child. Those who have needs are our customers, our employees and our friends.

Creating an approach to work together is the solution to the puzzle of safe, growing communities.

Xpose Hope has changed so many lives, and it has saved lives. But the work that we do could not have happened without our donor and volunteer base. We exist because others simply cared.

What changes will happen when your company takes an organized approach to giving—or your nonprofit reaches out in earnest to the community around it to encourage, network, and appreciate?

Melala Yousafzai, a Pakistani woman who was a human rights and women's education advocate once said, "Let us make our future now, and let us make our dreams tomorrow's reality."

What dreams can we create, together?

Acknowledgments

I am forever grateful to have had not one, but two amazing men who encouraged me to write, and who have stood by me as I worked pumping out words, many of which I'm sure ended up lining birdcages. To Layne and Tony, two amazing men, who both put up with more of me when I'm in the battle of finding the right word than I care to admit...are deserving of my admiration. And of course, I must acknowledge my children, who when I was writing full time, learned to hush when mommy had her headset on, and never talk to mommy when she was on a deadline.

This particular book could not have happened without my amazing business network partners. Each of them shared something of themselves and their businesses with me. All of them changed the way I looked upon business, both for profit and nonprofit. I would begin to list each of them, but I am sure I would forget many, through my own limitations, not due to them pouring any less into me.

Networking is much like knitting your own family. You begin hoping to shore up your own little kingdom, but before long, you are cheering for other kingdoms, even those who are in direct competition with you sometimes, to win. It's because inside most of us is an urge to better the world, and we know we can't do it all alone. If you aren't networking, you are missing some of the true nuggets of gold in this life.

I am grateful to those nonprofits that share the network space with me, often making my load less heavy. We work together, and we support one another in the task of simply changing one life here, and one life there, for the better. The bravado it takes to step out of the corporate world into the world of donations, auctions and service cannot be over emphasized. I applaud each of them, but in particular, Mike and Caryn Cross, with Free On the Outside Ministries who taught me so much about what it was to house another human being. These people stepped out into a world not often broached even by churches— that of the sex offender, and ended up helping my clients, as well.

To Tanya Hawkins, with Gung Ho Ministries, who not only provides for the needs of veterans in our community but also lovingly will dress any woman or man I send her, treating them as if they have come to the highest end designer shop. Giving dignity is a gift that can't be acknowledged enough.

To Cassie Greer, of Bag&Baggage Productions, who when the world was perhaps at its darkest for nonprofits, stepped forward to offer what she had to other charities. At a time when she could have horded her assets and donors, she opened them up to others. What an amazing human being she is.

To Elisa Joy "E.J." Payne. Elisa, much like Cassie, was barely holding on to her limited funding, at a point when none of us knew if more would ever come in, and she assisted others by allowing us to participate in gift wrap booths sponsored by the Hillsboro Downtown Partnership. By giving, she gained as people came downtown for wrapping and indeed, purchased more gifts!

To Ronette Fritts with Hope 4 Widows and Orphans, who sees beyond the general description of a widow and orphan to those who are without the support of others. Thank you for thinking of us.

And to all those who I don't work with as frequently who still care for our clients and for other nonprofits in so many ways—those who see beyond the general "give me" attitude of our sector to a vision of a community working together.

Thank you to every organization that assists nonprofits in their efforts to connect. From a small networking group above a daycare center, to the amazing businesses at All About Business Network (created by Xpose Hope), and my local chamber. Thank you to BNI® for living their "giver's gain" philosophy, and offering free one-year memberships to nonprofits during COVID. What a world changing donation that became!

And of course, I cannot begin to thank my coach, Darcey Edwards who pushed me to begin this book, as well as coach Richard Zielke, with whom the idea for this book began, and my editor, Tammy Moore, who takes my writing, and tweaks it just enough to take it from acceptable to amazing.

Thank you for helping me to change the community, the country, and the world.

About Betty

Betty Campbell is a former writer, fashion editor and contributing editor, as well as a successful entrepreneur.

Currently, she is the founder and executive director of Xpose Hope, a nonprofit that reaches trafficked persons and those in adult entertainment. Xpose Hope is currently operating in four states.

Connect with Betty

www.BettyLCampbell.com
www.xposehope.com
www.facebook.com/AuthorBettyCampbell
www.linkedin.com/in/betty-campbell-22677044
www.instagram.com/bettycampbellauthor

Work with Betty

Is your giving haphazard?

Do you think you are giving a lot but getting back very little other than a tax deduction?

Betty can provide a Legacy Report for your business, detailing community nonprofit organizations that fulfill the three keys covered in *Symbiotic Business.*

Betty is available to consult with your company, and help streamline, and empower your giving to push your company forward.

Nonprofits who wish to learn how to network within the business community and grow their donor and volunteer base can connect with Betty for consultations, as well.

To book a consultation or book Betty to speak to your association or business visit: www.BettyLCampbell.com

Made.in the USA
Las Vegas, NV
02 September 2021